1001 English Expressions and Phrases:

Common Sentences and Dialogues Used by Native English Speakers in Real-Life Situations

Jackie Bolen

Table of Contents

About the Author: Jackie Bolen

I taught English in South Korea for 10 years to every level and type of student. I've taught every age from kindergarten kids to adults. Most of my time has centered around teaching at two universities: five years at a science and engineering school in Cheonan, and four years at a major university in Busan where I taught upper level classes for students majoring in English. In my spare time, you can usually find me outside surfing, biking, hiking, or snowshoeing. I now live in Vancouver, Canada.

In case you were wondering what my academic qualifications are, I hold a Master of Arts in Psychology. During my time in Korea I successfully completed both the Cambridge CELTA and DELTA certification programs. With the combination of almost ten years teaching ESL/EFL learners of all ages and levels, and the more formal teaching qualifications I've obtained, I have a solid foundation on which to offer advice to English learners.

I truly hope that you find this book useful. I would love it if you sent me an email with any questions or feedback that you might have.

Jackie Bolen (www.jackiebolen.com)

Twitter: @bolen_jackie

Email: jb.business.online@gmail.com

You might also be interested in this book: Advanced English Conversation Dialogues. It has hundreds of helpful English idioms and expressions. Learn to speak more fluently in American English. You can find it wherever you like to buy books.

Good Manners and Greetings

Thank People

Thanks for your help today.

You're welcome.

I appreciate your help.

No problem.

Of course.

Thanks for (looking after my son, carrying my bag, helping me with my homework, etc.)

No worries.

That's very kind of you.

Oh, it was nothing.

No problem.

My pleasure.

You shouldn't have gone to the trouble.

It was no problem at all.

I was happy to help.

Thank you for _____ (many answers possible).

You're welcome.

You're the best!

Oh, thank you.

Dialogue #1:

Tom: Thanks for your help with moving today, Jenny. You shouldn't have gone to the trouble.

Jenny: Oh, no problem at all. I don't mind helping you. You've been very kind to me over the years.

Tom: You're welcome. And, I still really appreciate the help.

Jenny: No worries. That's what friends are for.

Dialogue #2:

Tim: Carrie, I really appreciate your help with that assignment.

Carrie: No problem, it was a tough one.

Tim: Yeah, I just couldn't figure it out.

Carrie: It took me a while too. Anyway, I'm always happy to help a friend out.

Tim: I'm thankful to have you in this class with me.

Greet Someone

Good morning (afternoon/evening).

Good morning/afternoon/evening.

Hi, how are you?

Good. How about you?

How are you doing?

Not bad. How about you?

What's up? (Very informal)

Oh, not much.

What have you been up to?

Nothing much. What about you?

Long time no see.

It has been a while!

Yeah, what have you been up to?

How's your day going?

Oh, pretty good. How about you?

Good to see you!

You too.

Dialogue #1:

Tom: Good morning Jenny. What you have been up to lately? We haven't talked in a while.

Jenny: Oh nothing much. Same old, same old. How about you?

Tom: Same here. Just really busy at work these days.

Jenny: Isn't everybody?

Dialogue #2:

Tim: Carrie! Long time, no see.

Carrie: Wow, it has been a while, right? Maybe a year?

Tim: Yeah, I think it was around Christmas last year that I ran into you at the mall.

Carrie: That's right. I remember that.

Tim: Anyway, nice to see you again!

Carrie: For sure. Let's catch up over coffee soon.

Say Goodbye and Finishing a Conversation

I gotta run. (Very informal)

Okay, talk to you later.

Let's chat later, okay?

Sure, sounds good.

Yeah, let's catch up again next week.

I need to get back to work.

I do too!

Can we talk more about this tomorrow?

Sure, no problem.

Of course.

See you later.

Okay.

I'm off now.

Okay, catch you later.

I gotta get going.

Sure, I'll see you later.

Dialogue #1:

Tom: Hey Jenny, I'm afraid that I gotta run. Can we talk more about this tomorrow?

Jenny: Sure, sounds good. I need to get back to work too.

Tom: Okay, chat later my friend.

Jenny: Sure.

Dialogue #2:

Tim: So, I think I need to get back to work.

Carrie: Oh, me too! That newsletter isn't going to write itself.

Tim: I know, right? Same with my report.

Carrie: We don't get paid the big bucks for nothing!

Say Sorry

Sorry to have kept you waiting.

Oh, it's fine. You're not that late.

It's okay. Don't worry about it.

Sorry I'm late.

Please don't let it happen again. (To a student or child.)

No problem.

I'm sorry for missing your message.

It's okay. I'm happy that I got a hold of you.

Excuse me, please/Pardon me.

Sure, no problem.

Sorry for bumping into you.

No worries.

My apologies for _____ (many answers possible).

It's okay.

My bad. (Very informal)

No problem.

Dialogue #1:

Tom: Oh hey Jenny. Sorry to have kept you waiting.

Jenny: No worries, you're not that late. My daughter was an hour late for our meeting yesterday. She said she missed my message about the time change.

Tom: Oh wow! What did you do?

Jenny: I said that I hoped it wouldn't happen again.

Dialogue #2:

Tim: My bad. Sorry for not finishing my part of the assignment on time.

Carrie: You put us in a tough spot.

Tim: I'm really sorry. How can I make it up to you?

Carrie: I think that if you finish your part by tomorrow morning, we can still turn it in on time.

Tim: Okay. I won't go to sleep until it's done.

Carrie: Okay.

Ask for Permission

Can I turn the TV on?

Oh sure, no problem.

Actually, I'd rather listen to music I think.

Do you mind if I turn up the music?

No, go ahead.

It's already quite loud!

Is it okay if I take the car to school tomorrow?

No, sorry. I need it for work.

Sure, no problem.

I'm planning on staying at my friend's house tonight? What do you think?

That's fine.

Don't you have school tomorrow?

Can I turn in my assignment three days late?

No, the deadline can't be changed.

Maybe, why do you need to?

Would it be all right if I took a look at your notes?

Sure, no problem.

Oh, they're so messy.

Dialogue #1:

Tom: Do you mind if I turn up the music? I can't hear that well in my old age!

Jenny: No, go ahead. It's fine with me.

Tom: And, I'd love to turn the heat up a bit too. It's freezing in here.

Jenny: Oh Tom, so many problems!

Dialogue #2:

Tim: Hey Mom, can I stay at Tony's house tonight?

Carrie: Are his parents going to be home?

Tim: Of course.

Carrie: It is a school night though, right?

Tim: No, remember it's a holiday tomorrow.

Carrie: Oh, that's right. Sure, you can. I'll just give his parents a quick call first though.

Ask for Help

Could you open the window/door, please?

Sure.

Of course.

Certainly.

Could you make me a cup of tea, please?

No problem.

Could you please give me a hand?

Sure, what do you need?

Could you look after my daughter this weekend for a couple of hours?

Sorry, I can't. I'm really busy.

Yes, I can.

Do you mind moving so that we could sit together?

Oh sure, no problem.

Do you have a few extra dollars to spare?

Sorry, I'm flat broke.

Sure, what's going on?

Do you have an extra pen I could borrow?

Sorry, I only have this one.

Yes, here you go.

Dialogue #1:

Tom: Could you please give me a hand this weekend?

Jenny: Sure, what do you need?

Tom: Would you mind looking after Tony during my dentist appointment?

Jenny: Okay, no problem. I love hanging out with him. What time?

Tom: From 2 until around 4.

Dialogue #2:

Tim: Oh hi, excuse me. Do you mind moving over one seat so that my friend and I could sit together?

Carrie: Sure, no problem.

Tim: Thanks so much.

Carrie: Of course, enjoy the movie.

Offer Help

Do you need a hand?

Sure, I'd love some help.

I just don't understand it!

I can explain it to you.

Do you want me to pick you up?

No, it's okay. My Dad said he would.

Yeah, that'd be great.

Do you have a ride home from the airport?

No, I don't. I'd love one. Or, I can take a taxi.

Yes, I already booked a ride-sharing service.

Do you want me to have a look at it?

Sure, that'd be great.

Yes, please.

What can I do for you?/How may I help you?

I'd love to look at that ring, please.

Can you please tell me the difference between these two computers?

I'm wondering how much this costs.

Could you please get me _____?

Dialogue #1:

Tom: Hey Jenny, do you need a ride to the airport?

Jenny: Oh, if you wouldn't mind. I'd appreciate it.

Tom: Sure, I don't mind lending you a hand.

Jenny: Thank you. I'll let you know my flight time once it's confirmed.

Dialogue #2:

Tim: Hi there, what can I do for you?

Carrie: I want to buy a new laptop but I'm not sure which one to get.

Tim: Sure. What's your budget?

Carrie: Not more than $1000.

Tim: Okay, there are three that I recommend taking a look at.

Carrie: Great. Can you walk me through their features?

Suggest an Idea

Let's open the window. It's so hot in here!

Good idea.

Oh, I have the air conditioning on. I'll just turn it up a little bit for you.

Why don't we ask my Mom to look after Jenny this weekend?

That's a great idea.

Oh, she's going camping this weekend with her friends.

How about taking the subway there?

I'd prefer to drive. It's so crowded at this time of day.

Sounds good.

What about checking out that new Italian place tonight?

Sounds great.

I just had Italian last night. What about Chinese?

Can we stop going out so much? I'm short on cash these days.

Oh definitely. Let's eat at home tonight.

I'd recommend checking out Stanley Park when you go to Vancouver.

Thank you. I'll have a look at that.

Have you thought about just getting a new computer?

Yeah, I have but they're so expensive. I'm hoping to just fix this one.

Oh really? That might be something to consider.

Dialogue #1:

Tom: I want to do something fun this weekend! Why don't we ask your parents to look after Tony?

Jenny: That's a great idea. How about checking out that new Greek restaurant?

Tom: Sounds good. I'll give your parents a call and see what they say.

Jenny: Perfect.

Dialogue #2:

Tim: Hey Carrie, do you want to catch a movie this weekend?

Carrie: Honestly, I'm a little short on cash these days. How about staying in and watching a movie at my house?

Tim: Sure, that sounds great too. There's this new one that just came out on Netflix that everyone is talking about.

Carrie: Awesome! I'll make some snacks for us. Come over at 7:30.

Give or Accept a Compliment

Your dinner was delicious!

Oh, I'm glad you liked it.

Thanks, it was a new recipe that I wanted to try.

That's a nice sweater.

Thank you.

You like it? I just bought it the other day.

Your presentation was so helpful.

That's good to hear.

You look really nice tonight.

Thanks, I appreciate you saying that.

What a lovely ring.

Thanks for noticing.

That color looks great on you.

Thanks.

Dialogue:

Tom: Hey Jenny, you look really nice tonight.

Jenny: Thanks so much. I appreciate you saying that.

Tom: Yes, I think it's your new haircut. It looks great.

Jenny: Oh wow. You're too kind.

How to Agree

I think Kobe Bryant was the best basketball player of my lifetime.

For sure!

Pizza is the world's most perfect food.

Most definitely.

He isn't an honest guy.

I think that's common knowledge.

I think the Oilers are going to win the Stanley Cup this year.

Yeah, you're probably right.

Let's get sushi tonight.

That's a great idea.

I'm so happy that Joe Biden won the US election.
I couldn't agree more.

I think we should see a movie tonight.

I can get on board with that.

Dialogue:

Tom: I know you don't love pizza, but that new restaurant is just so delicious.

Jenny: For sure. It's some of the best pizza I've ever had.

Tom: I'm so happy you liked it. And that movie we saw after? Amazing.

Jenny: Most definitely. It's going to win a ton of awards.

How to Disagree

Trump is going to win the election.

I don't think so.

I beg to differ.

Italian food is the ultimate!

Really? I prefer Greek.

That new job is way better.

I'm not sure about that.

Not necessarily. What about the amount of vacation time?

I loved that movie.

I didn't think it was that great.

It was okay but not amazing.

I'd love to go hiking this weekend.

Hmm...I think it's going to be pretty rainy!

The weather doesn't seem great.

Dialogue:

Tom: You should apply for the job. It's way better than your old one.

Jenny: I'm not so sure about that. The pay is better but it's only two weeks vacation.

Tom: Are you sure? Ken works there and has four weeks' I think.

Jenny: I'm pretty sure it's just two weeks when starting out. For the first 3 years.

How to Sympathize

My grandfather had a heart attack last night.

Oh, that's terrible.

I'm here for you if you want to talk.

My back hurts so much.

Sorry to hear that. Anything I can do to help?

I lost my jacket.

Let me help you look for it.

When did you last have it?

I've wasted half an hour looking for my car keys.

Oh no!

Can I help you look for them?

I have a really bad cold.

Take care of yourself, okay?

Please let me know if you need anything.

My boyfriend just broke up with me.

Oh no, please let me know if you want to talk.

Let's get some ice cream, okay?

Dialogue #1:

Tom: I got some sad news last night. I heard that my grandmother died.

Jenny: Oh no, I'm so sorry to hear that.

Tom: Yes, me too. We weren't that close but I'll miss her.

Jenny: Anything I can do to help? Want to grab a coffee and talk?

Dialogue #2:

Tim: Do you want to go for a quick hike after work today?

Carrie: Oh, I can't. I have a terrible cold.

Tim: Oh no! Did you stay home from work today?

Carrie: Yes. For the past three days actually.

Tim: Oh friend. That's terrible. Do you need me to bring you anything?

Carrie: My Mom brought me over some homemade soup. I'm doing okay.

Good Manners and Greetings Review

Write an appropriate response to each statement or question.

I really appreciate your help today.

Response:

What's up?

Response:

I have the worst headache.

Response:

I love your sweater.

Response:

Why don't we open the window?

Response:

Do you need a hand with that?

Response:

Could you please drive me to the airport?

Response:

Let's talk later.

Response:

In Public Places

Fitness Club

Scan your membership card here, please.

Sure, no problem.

My card isn't working.

Let me take a look at it for you.

Let me try.

I'm interested in a membership.

Sure, I can tell you about all the options.

Where's the locker room?

It's over there, on your right.

Do you have any fitness classes?

Yes, here's the schedule.

No, sorry we don't.

What are your fitness goals?

I'd like to have more endurance.

I want to have bigger muscles!

I want to get in better shape.

I want to lose some weight.

Dialogue #1:

Tom: Can you please scan your card here?

Jenny: Sure. Oh, it doesn't seem to be working.

Tom: Let me take a look for you. It's actually expired. You'll have to renew your membership.

Jenny: Sure, what are all my options?

Dialogue #2:

Tim: Do you have any fitness classes scheduled?

Carrie: Yes, the classes are listed online or you can have a look here.

Tim: I'm most interested in spin classes. Do you have any of those?

Carrie: Yes, we do. There's at least one of those classes almost every day.

Tim: Great. How can I sign up?

Carrie: Online, or with me now.

Exchange Money

Can I exchange some money, please?

Of course. No problem. How much?

What currency would you like?

Euros, please.

Would you like big or small notes?

A mix of big and small bills, please.

Mostly small notes, please.

Sorry, we don't accept coins.

Oh, okay. Thank you.

Please sign here.

Sure.

Can you please show me your passport?

Okay.

Here's your money.

Thank you.

Dialogue:

Tom: Can I please exchange some money?

Jenny: Sure, how much and what currency?

Tom: I'd like to get Canadian dollars, please. $700.

Jenny: Okay, and can you please show me your passport as well?

Tom: Sure.

Jenny: Would you like a mix of big and small bills?

Tom: Yes, please. That sounds great.

Movie Theater

Can I please get two tickets for Batman?

Sure, no problem.

Sorry, the 7:00 viewing is sold out. Would you like tickets for the 8:00 show?

That sounds great. Thank you.

I'd like a large popcorn and a large Coke, please.

Sure.

Would you like to add some candy and make it a combo?

Where would you like to sit?

I'd like to sit in the back (middle/front/aisle).

Do you have assigned seating?

No, you can sit anywhere you want.

Yes, where would you like to sit?

What size would you like?

A small (medium, large) please.

Anything else?

Sure, I'll have a medium coke.

No, that's it. Thank you.

Dialogue #1:

Tom: Hi, can I get four tickets for James Bond, please?

Jenny: Sure, the 7:30 viewing?

Tom: Yes, please. And do you have any combos that include popcorn and drinks?

Jenny: We do, but you don't buy them here. You can purchase them at the concession.

Tom: Okay, thank you.

Dialogue #2:

Tim: Can I see your ticket please?

Carrie: Here you go.

Tim: For the 8:00? You have to wait a few more minutes before going in.

Carrie: Oh really? Okay.

Library

Do you have your library card?

Yes, just a second.

How many books can I take out?

You can take out 10 books at a time.

When are they due?

They are due in two weeks.

Is there a quiet study space?

Yes, it's in the room at the back.

Where's the bathroom?

It's downstairs, on your left.

You have a late fine of $1.70. Would you like to pay for that now?

Yes, I can.

I lost my library card. Can I get a new one?

Sure, no problem.

Yes, but there's a $10 fee.

Dialogue #1:

Tom: Hi, it's my first time here. I just have a few questions.

Jenny: Sure, how can I help?

Tom: How many books can I take out at a time?

Jenny: You can take out up to 20 books.

Tom: And how long can I keep them?

Jenny: 3 weeks for books and 2 weeks for movies and music.

Tom: Finally, do you have a quiet study space?

Jenny: Unfortunately not but it's usually pretty quiet between 10 and 2.

Tom: Great, thanks for your help.

Dialogue #2:

Tim: I can't check these books out for some reason.

Carrie: Hmmm...let me take a look.

Tim: Oh, it says that you have overdue fees of $22 on your account. You can't take out more books if it's over $20.

Carrie: Really? I'll pay the fine now then.

Tim: Sure.

At the Bank

Can I please open an account?

Sure, what kind? Checking or savings?

Can I talk to someone about investment options?

Sure, let me check the schedule.

I'd like to exchange some money, please.

Sure, no problem.

I lost my ATM card.

Okay, do you have some ID?

You'll need to select a new PIN.

Okay.

Please sign here.

Sure.

I'd like to make a withdrawal, please.

Sure, how much?

Okay, from which account?

Dialogue #1:

Jenny: Hi, I'd like to open a new account.

Tom: Sure, checking or savings?

Jenny: A savings account, please.

Tom: Okay, do you have some ID?

Jenny: Yes, here's my driver's license.

Tom: Okay, I'll get that all set up for you. Sign here, please.

Dialogue #2:

Tim: I'm going to Europe and would like to get some Euros.

Carrie: Sure, how much?

Tim: €1000 Euros please.

Carrie: Sure, from your savings account?

Tim: Yes, please.

Carrie: Okay, let me get that for you.

Coffee Shop

Hi, what can I get you?

I'd like a medium drip coffee.

What size would you like?

A medium, (small, large, extra-large) please.

Would you like room?

Yes, please. (Room for cream or milk at the top).

Where can I find cream?

It's over there, by the door.

What time do you close?

We close at 9:00.

Do you have any food?

Yes, we have paninis and cookies.

No, sorry we don't.

Do you need anything else?

No thanks. That's it I think.

Do you have a points card?

No, I don't. Can I get one?

Yes, let me get it.

Dialogue #1:

Tom: Hi, what can I get you?

Jenny: I'd like a mint-chocolate chip Frappuccino, please.

Tom: Sure, what size would you like?

Jenny: Medium please. To go.

Tom: Sure.

Dialogue #2:

Tim: Hi, what would you like?

Carrie: What do you recommend? I don't really like coffee that much.

Tim: Do you want a hot or cold drink?

Carrie: Hot, please.

Tim: Sure, we have some nice teas or hot chocolate.

Carrie: Okay, I'll have a large hot chocolate then. For here.

At the Dentist

Have you had any problems with your teeth?

No.

Yes...

How often do you floss?

Once a week.

Every day.

Never.

How often do you brush?

3 times a day.

Only at night.

Can you feel that?

Yes/No.

Raise your arm if you have pain.

Okay.

Would you like to make another appointment now?

Yes, please.
No, I'll call later.

Do you have any benefits?

Yes, I do. I'll get the card.

No, I don't

Dialogue #1:

Dr. Thomsen: Hi Jenny, have you had any problems with your teeth?

Jenny: No, I think they're good.

Dr. Thomsen: Okay, let me have a look. Please raise your arm if you have any pain.

Jenny: Sure.

Dialogue #2:

Tim: How's your brushing and flossing going?

Carrie: I brush almost every time after I eat.

Tim: And your flossing?

Carrie: Well, not so great. Maybe once a week.

Tim: Okay. That's not ideal. You should be doing it every night before bed.

Carrie: I know. I'll do better.

In Public Places Review

Write an appropriate response to each statement or question.

Hi, what can I get you?

Response:

Please sign here.

Response:

Do you have your library card with you?

Response:

Please scan your card before going in.

Response:

Where would you like to sit?

Response:

How can I help you?

Response:

Do you need anything else?

Response:

Do you have any pain?

Response:

43

Interacting with People

Introduce Yourself or Someone Else

Hi, my name is Jackie.

Nice to meet you, I'm Julie.

What's your name?

My name is Jackie.

Who's this?

Oh, it's my friend Jenny.

This is my husband Kenny.

Nice to meet you.

Welcome to the party. My name is Jackie.

Thank you. My name is Tom.

Have you met my friend Julie before?

No, I don't think I have.

Dialogue:

Tom: Hi, I don't think we've met before. My name is Tom.

Jenny: Hi Tom. I'm Jenny. Nice to meet you.

Tom: Nice to meet you too.

Jenny: Oh, and this is my husband Kenny.

Tom: Nice to meet you, Kenny. I'm Tom.

Extend an Invite/Suggest an Idea

Would you like to have lunch together next week?

Sure, how about Thursday?

No, I can't. I'm so busy with this project. I have no free time.

Why don't we get a beer together after work?

Sorry, I'm busy tonight but how about tomorrow?

Yeah, I'd love to!

Are you interested in seeing the new James Bond movie with me?

That sounds great. How about this weekend?

Do you want to have dinner together on Friday?

Perfect.

I can't do Friday. How about Saturday?

I'm thinking about going to see the Rolling Stones concert. Are you interested?

Maybe. How much are the tickets?

Would you be interested in going hiking sometime?

Sure, I'd love to.

Hmmm...I don't really like exercising!

I don't like hiking but what about grabbing a beer?

Dialogue #1:

Tom: Do you have any plans this weekend? I'd love to see the new James Bond movie.

Jenny: Not really. Do you want to go together?

Tom: Yeah, that sounds great. And while we're making plans, are you interested in going to the U2 concert next month?

Jenny: I don't think I can do it. The tickets are so expensive.

Dialogue #2:

Tim: Let's grab a beer after work. I need to chill out.

Carrie: I know, it's been a long day. I'm game.

Tim: Awesome! Should we invite Bob and Jen?

Carrie: Sure, why not?

Tim: Okay, I'll ask them.

Carrie: Cool, let's walk over to the Dublin around 5:00.

Welcome Someone to your House

Thanks for coming over. Please come in.

Thanks for the invite.

Oh, thank you.

Welcome, make yourself at home.

Thank you.

Can I take your jacket?

Sure, thank you.

No, I'll keep it. I'm always cold.

Do I need to take my shoes off?

Yes, if you wouldn't mind.

No, don't worry about that.

I brought you a bottle of wine.

Thanks so much!

I'm so happy we could get together.

Me too! It's been a while.

Thanks for suggesting the idea.

Dialogue #1:

Tom: Hi Jenny! Thanks for coming over.

Jenny: Thanks so much for inviting me. I'm excited to see your home.

Tom: Please come in. Can I take your jacket?

Jenny: Sure, thank you. Should I take off my shoes?

Tom: Yes, if you don't mind.

Dialogue #2:

Tim: Welcome! Come on in.

Carrie: Thanks for having us over.

Tim: Of course. It's been a while.

Carrie: I know. Too long.

Tim: We need to do this more often.

Offer a Drink

Can I get you something to drink?

Sure, I'd love a glass of wine.

No thanks. I'm fine.

Do you want something to drink?

No, I'm okay. Thank you.

Yes, please.

Sure, what are you having?

What kind of beer do you have?

I have a lager, IPA, and cream ale.

Do you have any ciders?

Sure, I have some pear ones. Is that okay?

Would you like ice in your drink?

Yes, please.

No, thank you.

Dialogue:

Tom: Hi Jenny, would you like something to drink?

Jenny: Sure, what do you have?

Tom: Beer, wine, soda and water.

Jenny: I'll take a glass of wine, please. Red if you have.

Tom: Sure, coming right up.

Offer Food

Are you hungry?

No, I'm okay. I just ate dinner.

Yes, I'm famished.

Would you like something to eat?

Sure, I'd love something.

Do you want something salty or sweet?

I'm in the mood for sweet I think.

Can I grab you a snack?

Yes, please.

No, I'm okay.

Are you ready to eat?

Sure!

How about when the movie is over? I'm not that hungry yet.

Help yourself.

Sure, thank you.

Would you like a veggie burger or beef burger?

I'll have a veggie burger, please.

Dialogue #1:

Tom: Hey Jenny, are you hungry? I think I'm going to grab a snack.

Jenny: I am a little bit. What are you thinking?

Tom: Maybe something salty? Or are you in the mood for something sweet?

Jenny: Salty is great. How about some popcorn?

Tom: Sure, let's make some.

Dialogue #2:

Tim: So, I'm making burgers for dinner tonight. I have a few different kinds: beef, turkey, or veggie.

Carrie: Oh, what kind of veggie ones are they?

Tim: Some black bean ones that I got at Costco.

Carrie: Oh, those are delicious. I'll have one of those, please.

Tim: Good choice!

Compliment Someone on their Home

Your home is so lovely!

Thank you.

I love what you've done with your place. It's so beautiful.

Thanks. I appreciate it.

Your place looks so nice! Have you made some changes recently?

Yes, we painted since you were here last time.

Nothing special. We got some new plants though.

I love your couch! Where did you get it from?

From Ikea.

Where did you get this side table? It's lovely.

Oh, from Ikea.

Dialogue:

Tom: Hey Jenny. Please come in.

Jenny: Thank you. Oh wow...your home is lovely!

Tom: Thank you.

Jenny: I love the color of the walls and the couch too. It's perfect.

Tom: Thanks, I appreciate it.

Thank Someone for their Hospitality

Thanks so much for having me over. I appreciate it.

You're welcome. I'm happy you came over.

I loved all the food! Thank you.

You're welcome. I'm happy you enjoyed it.

Thanks for your hospitality. I'll have you over next time.

Sure, sounds good.

What a fabulous night. Thank you!

Yes, it was so nice to see you.

Dialogue:

Tom: Thanks so much for having me over Jenny. I had such a good time.

Jenny: You're welcome. It was so nice to see you.

Tom: And the food too. I can't forget about that. Everything was so delicious.

Jenny: Thank you.

Tom: I'll have you over next time, okay?

Jenny: Sure.

Interacting with People Review

Write an appropriate response to each statement or question.

Thanks for having me over for dinner.

Response:

Your house is so nice!

Response:

Would you like a drink?

Response:

Are you hungry yet?

Response:

Do you want to catch that concert with me next week?

Response:

Want to grab a drink after work?

Response:

Hi, my name is Jackie.

Response:

Welcome, please come in.

Response:

Dating

Ask Someone Out on a Date

Would you like to get dinner with me sometime?

Sure, that sounds great.

Can I get your phone number, please?

Sorry, I already have a girlfriend.

I'd love to take you out this weekend. Are you interested?

Yes, definitely.

I would love to get to know you more. Would you like to go out for dinner with me?

That sounds good.

I know this is a little forward, but I'd love to get coffee with you sometime.

I'd love to.

Dialogue:

Tom: I enjoyed talking to you and would love to get to know you more. Do you want to have dinner with me on Friday?

Jenny: That sounds great.

Tom: Okay, give me your number and we can make some more plans.

Jenny: Sure.

Refuse an Offer of a Date

Would you like to go out with me this weekend?

Sorry, I'm busy.

I'd love to take you out on a date.

Sorry, I already have a boyfriend (girlfriend).

Are you interested in having dinner with me on Friday?

I don't think that'll work. Sorry.

Do you want to grab dinner tomorrow night?

I'd love to but _____. (Only if you like the person!)

Dialogue:

Tom: I enjoyed talking to you. Are you interested in having dinner sometime next week?

Jenny: Oh, sorry I can't. I'm busy with work.

Tom: Oh too bad. How about some other time then?

Jenny: I've enjoyed chatting with you too but I don't think we're a good fit. Good luck on future dates.

Tom: Okay, well nice talking to you anyways!

How to Avoid Answering a Question

Tell me about your family.

Oh, there's not much to tell!

Tell me about your job.

Nothing interesting to say about that! Why don't you tell me about yours?

So, where did you grow up?

I moved around a lot. What about you?

Do you want to have children?

I haven't decided yet. What do you think about that?

Tell me about yourself.

Oh, what would you like to know?

Dialogue:

Tom: So Jenny, tell me about yourself.

Jenny: That's such a general question. What would you like to know?

Tom: What about your family?

Jenny: There's not much to tell. I just have one sister. How about you?

Tom: Similar to you.

Ask for Another Date

I had a really fun time and I'd love to see you again.

Me too, let's plan for next week?

I had a good time but I don't think this is going to work.

Are you interested in going out with me again?

Sorry, I don't feel the same way. Maybe just being friends is better?

That sounds nice.

Do you want to get dinner with me this weekend?

Sure, that sounds great.

I'd like to get to know you more. What do you think about that?

I'd love to as well.

I'm sorry. I don't think I'm interested.

Dialogue:

Tom: I had a really good time getting to know you. Are you interested in going out with me again?

Jenny: Yes, I'd love to. How about this weekend?

Tom: Sure, that sounds good. Let's text later on in the week to make plans.

Jenny: Perfect.

Dating Review

Write an appropriate response to each statement or question.

Can I get your phone number, please?

Response:

Would you like to go out with me next week?

Response:

I liked talking to you. Do you want to go out sometime?

Response:

I had a really good time. Can I see you again?

Response:

Tell me about yourself.

Response:

Tell me about your family.

Response:

Small Talk

Talk about the Weather

Wow, it's so cold outside!

Yeah, it's freezing.

I can't believe how much it's raining today!

I know, I'm so happy I remembered my umbrella.

Did you see the forecast? It's going to be sunny all next week.

Yes, I'm excited about it!

I can't wait.

Nice weather this weekend. Any big plans?

Oh, not really. I may do some work in the garden.

It's so sunny out there!

I know. I seriously regret not bringing my sunglasses.

Beautiful day, isn't it?

Yes, it is.

It feels like winter is coming.

Yeah, there's a chill in the air today.

Dialogue #1:

Tom: It's raining cats and dogs!

Jenny: Yeah, my feet are soaking wet. I hate it.

Tom: Did you see the forecast though? Lots of sun next week.

Jenny: I'm already looking forward to it.

Dialogue #2:

Tim: The weather looks great for this weekend. Do you have any plans?

Carrie: I'm going to get my garden ready for planting.

Tim: Yeah, it is that time of year, right? The days are getting longer.

Carrie: Definitely. What are you up to?

Tim: Probably going kayaking with a friend. That's about it.

Carrie: Okay, have fun.

Talk about Activities

What are you up to this weekend?

Oh, the usual. Going hiking and hanging out with my friends.

Did you go hiking this weekend?

The weather wasn't great so I didn't. But, I'll try to get out next weekend.

Yes, I went to Mount Seymour.

So what are some of your hobbies?

Well, I like to read, watch TV, and cook for friends.

It's going to be nice this weekend. Do you have any plans for getting outside?

For sure. My friend and I will go kayaking I think.

Not really. I'll try to go for a bike ride though.

Seen any interesting shows on Netflix lately?

Oh yeah, I loved _____ .

Did you do anything interesting this weekend?

Not much. I mostly just stayed in and watched TV. How about you?

I just got back from camping last night.

Dialogue #1:

Tom: Hey Jenny, what are you up to this weekend?

Jenny: Oh, not much. I think the weather is going to be terrible. Maybe some cooking and Netflix. How about you?

Tom: That sounds nice. I go hiking in all weather, so I'll probably do that on Saturday.

Jenny: Wow. You're braver than me!

Dialogue #2:

Tim: Did you get up to anything fun this weekend?

Carrie: Yeah, I went camping with my family.

Tim: Nice! Where did you go?

Carrie: We went to Porteau Cove. Our campsite was right on the ocean.

Tim: That sounds fabulous. I'd love to see some pictures.

Talk about the Local Sports Team

Did you see the game last night?

It was a real nail-biter!

No, I missed it. I had to work.

Do you follow the Kings?

I don't even know what sport they play!

Yeah, who doesn't in this city?

Did you hear that the Oilers are going to trade Connor McDavid?

Wow! Where did you hear that?

Are you excited about the upcoming NHL season?

For sure, I'll catch a few games. My boyfriend is obsessed with the Canucks.

I don't follow hockey.

That was a poor showing from the Oilers last night.

I know, they're having a terrible season this year.

Better than last year though!

Dialogue:

Tom: Hey, did you catch the game last night?

Jenny: Which one? I'm out of the loop.

Tom: The Canucks. They're in the playoffs now.

Jenny: Oh yeah, I did hear about that. Did they win?

Tom: They sure did!

Small Talk about the News

Did you catch the news last night?

Oh yeah, crazy, right?

No, I didn't hear anything. What happened?

Did you hear that the bus drivers might go on strike?

Really? Why?

Yeah, I heard that on the radio on my way to work.

I can't believe the election has finally been decided.

I know, right? It's been forever.

It's about time!

Did you hear about that big earthquake in Chile?

No, what happened?

I know. It's tragic.

Dialogue:

Tom: Did you catch the news last night?

Jenny: Oh no, what happened?

Tom: There was a huge flood in Florida.

Jenny: Oh wow. What happened?

Tom: There was a massive storm that they weren't prepared for.

Jenny: Oh, I'll have to take a look at it.

Small Talk at Work

So, have you worked here for a long time?

Not really. Just a few months.

Yeah, for about 5 years.

How's your week been so far?

Oh, pretty good. How about you?

Long but it's been okay.

What are you up to this weekend?

Not much, just recovering from the week.

I have to run some errands.

Did you see the new coffee machine we got?

No! I'll have to try it out.

Yeah, the coffee is delicious!

Are you looking forward to your vacation time?

Yes, I really need it!

I really need a break.

Yes, I'm going to Disneyland with my kids.

Dialogue #1:

Tom: Hi, I don't think we've met. I'm Tom.

Jenny: Hi, I'm Jenny. How long have you been working here?

Tom: Just a couple of weeks now. How about you?

Jenny: For a few years.

Dialogue #2:

Tim: Hey Carrie! Big news. We're getting a new espresso machine.

Carrie: Seriously? I've been bugging Tony about that for years now!

Tim: I know, right? It's coming next week.

Carrie: Wow! Work just got a whole lot better. I can stop wasting money at the coffee shop.

Small Talk Review

Write an appropriate response to each statement or question.

Did you see the game last night?

Response:

Wow, it's so hot outside today!

Response:

Did you do anything interesting this weekend?

Response:

It's raining cats and dogs today.

Response:

What are you doing this weekend?

Response:

Do you have a favourite NBA team?

Response:

Did you hear that the Cowboys made it to the Superbowl?

Response:

The forecast is all sun next week!

Response:

Shopping

Ask if a Shop Has Something You Need

Excuse me, do you have any _____?

Sorry, we don't.

Yes, they're over there.

Do you know where I can find _____?

Yes, it's down one floor and on the right.

I'm looking for this in a bigger size, please.

I can look in the back for you.

Do you have these shoes in a size 9?

Let me have a look. Just a minute.

I'm wondering if you have _____.

I'm not sure, let me check for you.

We just got some in. They're in aisle 7.

I hope you can help me. I'm looking for _____.

Sure, we have that in stock.

Oh sorry, we just sold out.

Dialogue #1:

Tom: Excuse me, I'm looking for the Air Jordans in a size 8.5.

Jenny: Hmmm...let me check for you. Just a second.

Tom: Sure.

Jenny: Okay, I see that we should have a couple of pairs. Let me grab one for you to try on.

Tom: Sure, that sounds great. Thank you.

Dialogue #2:

Tim: Hi, I'm looking for a sweater for my Mom. Do you have any recommendations?

Carrie: Sure, we have some nice ones on sale over there.

Tim: Great.

Carrie: Did you have a specific color in mind?

Tim: She really likes dark colors, black and grey.

Carrie: Okay, we have a few you can take a look at.

Buy Things

How much is this?

Let me check for you.

It's $7.20.

Do you have this sweater in a different color?

No, sorry, only the ones you can see on the shelf.

Yes, you can find more colors online.

Would you like a bag for that?

No, thank you. I have a bag already.

Yes, please.

Would you like that delivered?

Yes, please.

Do you want to get the extended warranty?

No, thank you.

Maybe, how must does it cost?

Is that with cash or credit card?

Credit card, please.

Sign here.

Sure, thank you.

Dialogue #1:

Tom: How much is this sweater? I don't see a price-tag.

Jenny: It's on sale for $29.99.

Tom: Great, thanks. Do you have any other colors?

Jenny: No, just the ones you see here.

Dialogue #2:

Tom: Hi, can I help you find something?

Jenny: Oh, I'm just browsing.

Tom: Okay, let me know if you need help.

Jenny: I will.

Return or Exchange Things

I'd like to return this, please.

Sure, is there something wrong with it?

Okay, no problem.

I'd like to exchange this, please.

Sure, what's the reason for it?

I bought this _____ but it doesn't work.

Oh, let me have a look.

I bought these shoes but they don't fit well.

Okay, would you like to try on a different size?

Do you have the card you bought it with?

Yes, it's right here.

No, can I get the money back to this other one?

Please insert your card into the machine.

Sure.

Oh, I don't have it with me right now.

What's your email?

It's _____.

Dialogue #1:

Tom: I'd like to exchange this t-shirt, please.

Jenny: Is there anything wrong with it?

Tom: Oh no, I bought it for my daughter but she doesn't like the color.

Jenny: Okay, I see. Would you like a refund or would you like to exchange it?

Tom: A refund is great.

Dialogue #2:

Tim: I'd like to get a refund, please.

Carrie: What's the problem with it?

Tim: Well, when I cut into it, it was already rotten. I just bought it this morning.

Carrie: Oh, sorry about that. Do you have the card you bought it with?

Tim: Yes, right here.

Carrie: Okay, I'll process the refund.

Buy Food

Could I please get some shaved roast beef?

Sure, how much would you like?

How would you like it sliced?

Thin, (thick, medium) please.

Do you have any more _____?

Sorry, we're all out right now.

I'm looking for some gluten-free pasta.

Sure, it's in aisle 7 on the right.

I'm allergic to nuts. Does this product contain any?

Let me check for you.

No, you're safe.

Could you please slice this bread for me?

Sure. How thick?

I'd like to order a cake for my son's birthday, please.

Sure, no problem.

Okay, would you like something written on it?

When would you like to pick it up?

Dialogue #1:

Tom: Hi, I'd like to get some shaved ham please.

Jenny: Sure, how much would you like?

Tom: 300 grams, please.

Jenny: And how would you like it sliced?

Tom: Thinly, please.

Jenny: Okay, I'll grab it for you.

Dialogue #2:

Tim: Hi, I'd like to order a cake, please.

Carrie: Sure, for when?

Tim: This Saturday.

Carrie: Sure, which one?

Tim: The large rectangle one, please.

Carrie: Okay, what would you like written on it?

Tim: Happy Birthday Molly.

Carrie: Okay, we'll have that ready for pick-up by 10 am on Saturday.

Buy Clothes

Can I try these on, please?

Sure.

There's a limit of 10 items in the change room.

Okay.

Do you have these in a bigger size?

Let me check for you.

Where can I try these on?

The change rooms are over there.

What's your return policy?

Within 30 days as long as you have the receipt.

Do you need a bag?

Yes, please.

Do you need any help finding anything?

No, thanks. I'm just browsing.

What style do you like?

(many answers)

Dialogue #1:

Tom: Hi, do you need any help finding something?

Jenny: Oh, maybe. I'm looking for some jeans.

Tom: Sure, what style do you like?

Jenny: Straight-leg, please.

Tom: Let's have a look over here. We have a couple of options.

Dialogue #2:

Tim: Can I try these on please?

Carrie: Sure, the changing room is over there.

Tim: Okay, thank you. How many items can I bring in?

Carrie. Only 5. But we can hold some outside for you.

Shopping Review

Write an appropriate response to each statement or question.

Cash or card?

Response:

Do you need help finding anything?

Response:

Would you like a bag for that?

Response:

It's a bit more than I wanted to spend.

Response:

What size do you need?

Response:

I'm looking for these in size 6.

Response:

What's your return policy?

Response:

Where can I try these on?

Response:

Getting Around Town

Take a Taxi

Can I get a taxi to _____ at _____?

Sure, no problem

I don't see the taxi yet. Is he still coming?

Yes, he's on the way.

Oh, he should be there now. You don't see him?

Can I go to _____?

Sure, no problem.

How much is it?

It'll be around $70.

Do you go to the airport?

Yes, do you want to go now?

No, you'll have to get a green taxi for that.

Do you want to put your bag in the trunk?

Sure.

No, it's okay. I'll keep it in the back seat with me.

Dialogue #1:

Tom: Where would you like to go?

Jenny: To the airport, please. Do you go there?

Tom: Yes I do.

Jenny: About how much will it cost?

Tom: Around $50.

Jenny: Okay. Sounds good.

Dialogue #2:

Tim: Where can I get a taxi to downtown?

Carrie: Oh, there's a taxi stand one block that way, on your right.

Tim: Perfect. Thank you.

Ask for and Give Directions

I think I'm lost. Can you tell me how to get to _____?

Sure, no problem.

Sorry, I don't know where that is either.

How can I get to _____?

Go straight for two blocks and it's on the right.

Is there a bus that goes to the airport from here?

Yes, the number 7. It leaves in about 30 minutes.

Do you know where this bookstore is?

Sorry, I'm not sure.

Oh, you're close. It's just a few hundred meters down the street that way.

Where exactly am I right now? I think I'm lost.

Oh, you're right by Granville Skytrain station. It's across the street.

Dialogue:

Tom: Excuse me, I think I'm lost. Do you know where the bus stop is?

Jenny: There are two near here. Where are you going?

Tom: To the airport.

Jenny: Okay, cross the street and walk one block. You'll have to take the number six.

Take the Train or Bus

Where are you going?

To Seoul.

What time would you like to leave?

At 9 pm.

Regular or deluxe seat?

Regular, please.

How much does each of them cost?

Sorry, we don't have any tickets left for that time. Would you like to go one hour later?

Sure, thank you.

No thanks. I'll take the train instead.

Do you need a receipt?

No, thank you.

Dialogue:

Tom: Where would you like to go?

Jenny: Busan, please.

Tom: Okay, leaving now?

Jenny: Yes, please.

Tom: Regular seat?

Jenny: Yes.

Tom: Okay, here's your ticket for the 8:20 train. You're at platform 3.

83

Car Rental

Do you have any cars available?

Yes, we do.

Sorry, not right now. We'll have some tomorrow.

What kind of car would you like?

A small SUV or van.

Do you need insurance?

No, thank you.

Yes, please. What are the options?

Please sign here.

Sure.

For how many days?

One week, please.

Can you check the car for any damage?

Okay.

Do you have a reservation?

Yes, I do.

No, I don't.

Dialogue #1:

Tom: Hi, I'd like to rent a car, please.

Jenny: Sure, for how long?

Tom: 5 days, please.

Jenny: Is a Toyota Corolla okay?

Tom: Yes, that's great.

Jenny: Do you need the optional insurance?

Tom: No thanks, I have some with my credit card already.

Dialogue #2:

Tim: Okay, here are your keys. Can you please check the car for damage?

Carrie: Okay. I see a bunch of scratches here.

Tim: Those ones? We already have note of those.

Carrie: Okay. Looks good besides that.

Tim: Good. Have a great trip.

Getting Around Town Review

Write an appropriate response to each statement or question.

What kind of car would you like?

Response:

Where would you like to go?

Response:

Sorry, I don't go there.

Response:

That bus is sold out.

Response:

Can you please tell me how to get to the library?

Response:

Excuse me, I think I'm lost. I'm looking for Room 123.

Response:

Would you like a window or aisle seat?

Response:

Regular or deluxe seat?

Response:

Air Travel

Check In

May I please see your passport?

Okay.

Here you go.

Would you like a window or aisle seat?

An aisle (window) seat, please.

Do you have any checked bags?

Yes, two of them.

Can you put them on the scale?

Okay.

Did you pack these bags yourself?

Yes.

Let me put a tag on them.

Okay.

What's your final destination?

Seoul, South Korea.

Dialogue:

Tom: Can I see your passport please?

Jenny: Sure

Tom: Do you have any bags to check?

Jenny: Yes, just one.

Tom: Okay, what's your final destination?

Jenny: Tokyo.

Tom: Please put your suitcase on the scale.

Jenny: Sure.

Tom: Did you pack the bag yourself?

Jenny: Yes.

Tom: Okay, here are your tickets. You're boarding at gate 3. Please be there by 10:20.

Jenny: Thank you.

Go Through Security

Can you please have your ID and boarding pass ready?

Sure.

Please show me your boarding pass.

Okay.

Put your bags on the belt.

Okay.

Do you have a computer or laptop in the bag?

Yes/No.

Please take it out.

Sure.

Please come through.

Okay.

Do you have anything in your pockets?

Oh, just a second. I think I do.

No, I don't.

Let me check.

Dialogue:

Tom: Please show me your boarding pass.

Jenny: Okay.

Tom: Do you have a computer or phone in the bag?

Jenny: Yes.

Tom: Please take it out and put it into a separate bin.

Jenny: Okay.

Tom: Please come through. Hold out your arms.

Jenny: Sure.

Tom: Do you have anything in your pockets?

Jenny: Just a second. Let me check.

Go Through Immigration

Where are you staying?

With my friend.

What's their address?

_____.

Please show me your passport.

Okay.

What's the purpose of your visit?

I'm attending a conference.

I'm here for business.

I'm travelling.

How long are you staying for?

2 weeks.

Do you have a return ticket?

Yes, would you like to see it?

No, I'm travelling by land to Thailand. Then flying home from there.

Do you have anything to declare?

Yes, I do.

No, I don't.

Dialogue #1:

Tom: Please show me your passport.

Jenny: Okay.

Tom: What's the purpose of your visit?

Jenny: I'm visiting my friend.

Tom: How long are you staying?

Jenny: 3 weeks.

Tom: Okay, have a good visit.

Dialogue #2:

Tim: What's the purpose of your visit?

Carrie: I'm here for a business conference.

Tim: Okay, how long are you staying?

Carrie: For 3 days.

Tim: Can I see your passport?

Carrie: Sure.

Tim: Okay, have a good trip.

Report Lost Luggage

Excuse me, where can I report lost luggage?

Over there, by the exit.

Excuse me, I didn't see my bag on the carousel.

Okay, what's your flight?

What color is your bag?

It's a small green one.

Do you have your baggage tag?

Yes, I do. Here you go.

Where are you staying?

At Hotel ABC.

What's your phone number?

It's 778-743-7214.

Dialogue:

Tom: Excuse me, I didn't see my bag on the carousel.

Jenny: Okay, please show me your baggage tag.

Tom: Sure.

Jenny: You were at carousel 3? You checked for it there?

Tom: Yes.

Jenny: Okay, let's get this sorted out for you.

Air Travel Review

Write an appropriate response to each statement or question.

Can I see your passport, please?

Response:

Are you checking any bags?

Response:

Did you pack the bag yourself?

Response:

Where are you staying?

Response:

What's the purpose of your visit?

Response:

How long are you staying for?

Response:

Do you have your boarding pass ready?

Response:

Staying in a Hotel

Check In and Check Out

Hi, I'd like check in, please.

Sure, what's your name?

Do you have a reservation?

No, do you have any rooms available?

Yes, I do.

I'd like to check out, please.

Sure, let me get your name.

You have a charge of $376. How would you like to pay for that?

With the credit card on file.

Can I extend my stay for 1 night, please?

Sure, let me check if we have rooms available.

Oh, sorry. We're all booked up.

Can I get an extra key, please?

Okay. Just one more?

Sorry, we only allow two keys per room.

Dialogue #1:

Tom: Hi, I'd like to check in, please.

Jenny: Sure, do you have a reservation?

Tom: Yes, it's under Tom Smith.

Jenny: Okay, let me check. Oh, there it is.

Tom: Great.

Dialogue #2:

Tim: Hi, I'd like to check out please.

Carrie: Sure, what's your room number?

Tim: 301.

Carrie: Okay, everything looks good. Do you have the four keys?

Tim: Yes, here you go.

Carrie: Great. Have a safe drive.

Make a Complaint

My room is very noisy. Are there other ones available?

Sure, let me have a look.

People were swimming in the pool past 10 pm. It was very loud in my room.

Oh, sorry about that.

I think the people in the next room are smoking. Isn't this a non-smoking hotel?

Oh really? Would you like to change rooms?

Someone is parked in my parking spot.

Oh, okay. Sorry about that. Let's get that fixed.

I'm allergic to dogs and I think someone with a dog was staying in the room before me.

Oh no! Let's see if I can find you another room.

The WiFi doesn't seem to be working in my room.

Okay, do you want me to have a look at your device? Do you have it here?

Dialogue #1:

Tom: Hi, my room is really loud! It was difficult to sleep last night.

Jenny: What was the problem?

Tom: The noise from the street. There was so much traffic.

Jenny: I'll check if there's a room on the other side of the building.

Tom: Thank you.

Dialogue #2:

Tim: I can't get the WiFi to work in my room.

Carrie: Okay, were you able to connect at all?

Tim: No, I couldn't figure out the network and password.

Carrie: Do you have your device here? I can give it a try.

Tim: Sure, thank you.

Carrie: Okay, you should be good to go now.

Tim: Thank you.

Ask About Amenities

Excuse me. Do you have a pool or hot tub here?

No, sorry we don't.

Where can I find the ice machine?

It's on the second floor, next to the elevator.

Do you have a fitness center?

Yes, it's on the third floor.

Do you have room service available?

No, we don't have a restaurant here. But, you can order food from Uber Eats.

Yes, the menu should be in your room.

Can someone clean my room when I'm gone today?

Sure, just leave the tag on your door when you go.

Can I please get a wake-up call at 7:20?

Sure, I'll set that up.

I need to print something off. Can I do that here?

Yes, I can help you with that.

Yes, we have a business center down the hall with a printer.

99

Dialogue #1:

Tom: Excuse me, do you have a pool here?

Jenny: Yes, it's on the first floor.

Tom: Okay, what time does it close?

Jenny: At 10 pm.

Tom: Where can I find pool towels?

Jenny: They're in your room, in the closet.

Tom: Okay, thank you.

Dialogue #2:

Tim: I'm wondering if you have room service available?

Carrie: Yes, from 7 am to 9 pm.

Tim: Okay, great. Where can I see the menu?

Carrie: It's in the information book on the desk in your room.

Tim: Perfect, thank you.

Carrie: All the instructions for how to order it are there.

Staying in a Hotel Review

Write an appropriate response to each statement or question.

Excuse me, where can I find the fitness center?

Response:

Do you have a reservation?

Response:

Would you like to change rooms?

Response:

I'd like to check out, please.

Response:

Can you please tell your name and room number?

Response:

Do you have a restaurant here?

Response:

At the Doctor's Office

Make an Appointment

I'd like to make an appointment, please.

Sure, for when?

Have you been here before?

Yes, I have.

No, I'm a new patient.

Which doctor would you like to see?

Dr. Brown, please.

What's the problem?

(many answers)

Do you prefer morning or afternoon?

Morning.

Are you available later today?

Yes, but only after 3.

No, tomorrow is better I think.

Dialogue:

Tom: Can I make an appointment for tomorrow please?

Jenny: Sure, with which doctor?

Tom: Dr. Brown.

Jenny: We have nothing tomorrow but how about Wednesday?

Tom: Sure, that's fine.

Jenny: Okay, I'll put you in for 2:00?

Tom: Sounds good.

Jenny: What are you coming in for?

Tom: I have a sore toe.

Jenny: Okay, we'll see you on Wednesday.

Cancel or Change an Appointment

Hi, I'd like to cancel my appointment, please.

Sure, what's your name?

I have an appointment at 3:00 but I'm going to be late. Is it okay to come at 3:30 instead?

Sure, no problem. The doctor is running behind anyway.

No, it's not possible. Would you like to reschedule?

Can I please change my appointment to tomorrow?

Sure, what time?

Sorry, there are no appointments for tomorrow.

Would it be possible to meet next Tuesday?

That's fine. What time?

I can't but how about Thursday?

Are you free to meet on Friday instead?

Sure, that'll work.

Dialogue:

Tom: Hi, this is Tom. I have an appointment at 3:00 but I won't be able to make it.

Jenny: Okay, do you need to reschedule?

Tom: Yes, please. Do you have anything for Thursday?

Jenny: Yes, how about 2:30?

Tom: Sounds good. Thank you.

With the Doctor

What brings you here today?

(many answers: describe the problem).

How long has this been happening?

For 2 months.

It just started recently.

Do you have any pain?

Not really.

Yes, it hurts a lot, especially at night.

Do you have lots of stress right now?

Not really, just the normal things.

Yes, I just moved and lost my job as well.

Do I need to make another appointment?

Come back in 2 weeks if you're not better.

Yes, I'd like to see you in 1 week from now.

We need to run some tests.

Okay.

Dialogue #1:

Tom: Hi Jenny, what brings you here today?

Jenny: I have this strange rash on my arm.

Tom: How long have you had it?

Jenny: For 6 months now.

Tom: Okay, is it itchy?

Jenny: Mostly at night.

Tom: I'm going to prescribe this cream. Let's see if that clears it up. Come back in a month if that doesn't work.

Dialogue #2:

Tim: Hi Carrie, what can I help you with today?

Carrie: I've been having lots of stomachaches lately.

Tim: I see. Have you changed your diet recently?

Carrie: No, just the usual.

Tim: What about stress? Any big thing coming up?

Carrie: Yes, actually I just changed jobs. I'm having trouble sleeping too.

Tim: Do you think that might be the cause of it?

At the Doctor's Office Review

Write an appropriate response to each statement or question.

What brings you in today?

Response:

Which doctor would you like to see?

Response:

How long has this been going on?

Response:

I'd like to change my appointment:

Response:

What time would you like to come in?

Response:

We have openings at 3:00 and 4:30.

Response:

What's the problem?

Response:

Eating Out

Make a Reservation

I'd like to make a reservation, please.

Sure, for what day and time?

How many people?

7.

I have a reservation for 4:00 but I'd like to change it to 6:00, please.

No problem.

Sorry, we're full at 6:00. How about 5:00?

Do you take reservations?

Sorry, we don't.

Yes, but you have to book online.

It'll be about a 30-minute wait.

Okay, we'll wait.

We'll go somewhere else. Thank you.

Dialogue:

Tom: I'd like to make a reservation for tomorrow at 6.

Jenny: Sure, for how many people?

Tom: 6.

Jenny: Okay, what's your name and phone number?

Tom: It's Tom and my number is 604-773-9437.

Meet Friends Already in the Restaurant

Hi, I'm meeting some friends here.

Okay, did they have a reservation?

I'm meeting some people here but I'm not sure if they're here yet.

I think they might be sitting over there.

Oh, your table isn't quite ready yet.

Hi, my friends are here but I'm not sure where they are.

Do you want to have a look around? Go ahead.

Dialogue:

Tom: Hi, I'm supposed to be meeting some people but I'm not sure if they're here yet.

Jenny: Okay, do you have a reservation?

Tom: Yes, under Kenny.

Jenny: Ah, okay. You're over here. Follow me.

Tom: Thank you.

Make an Order

Would you like a drink to start with?

I'll have a beer.

No thanks, water is fine.

I haven't decided yet. Give me a minute, please.

Would you like something to start with?

Sure, I'll have the Caesar salad.

No thank you. I'll go with the Clubhouse sandwich.

What can I get you?

I'll have _____.

Are you interested in dessert?

Can I see the menu?

No thanks, I'm so full!

Do you have any specials tonight?

Yes, they are_____.

I can't decide between the tomato pasta and the creamy lasagna. What do you think?

I personally love the lasagna here.

Dialogue #1:

Tom: Hi, can I get you something to drink?

Jenny: I'd love a glass of red wine and I'm ready to order too.

Tom: Sure, what would you like?

Jenny: I'll have the lasagna, please.

Tom: Okay, that's a great choice.

Jenny: I hope so!

Dialogue #2:

Tim: Are you ready to order?

Carrie: Not quite yet. Can you give us another minute?

Tim: Sure, no problem. Can I start you off with a drink though?

Carrie: Okay, I'll have a pint of your house lager please.

Tim: Okay, I'll be right back.

Make a Special Request

Can I please take the rest to go?

No problem. I'll pack it up for you.

I'm allergic to gluten. Do you have any recommendations?

We can make any of the pasta dishes with gluten-free noodles.

I'm allergic to garlic. Does the creamy pasta sauce have garlic in it?

I'm not sure. I'll check with the chef.

It's safe! The tomato sauce has garlic but not the cream one.

I'm a vegan and am wondering what my options are?

We can make almost anything on the menu vegan. What are you interested in?

We're going to share the meal. Can you please cut the burger in half?

Sure, no problem.

Can I get an extra plate, please?

I'll grab you one.

I dropped my napkin on the floor. Could I please get another one?

No problem.

Could I have more ketchup, please?

Sure, I'll bring that right over.

Dialogue:

Tom: What can I get you?

Jenny: I'm thinking about the teriyaki rice bowl but I'm vegan.

Tom: We can do that with with tofu instead of chicken if you like.

Jenny: Really? That'd be great. I'll have that, please. It's gluten-free, right?

Tom: Yes, it is. I'll write it on the order too just to be sure.

Dialogue #2:

Tim: Excuse me, could I please get some more ketchup for my fries?

Carrie: Sure, no problem.

Tim: Oh, and some hot sauce too.

Carrie: Okay.

Tim: Thank you! Sorry to be such a hassle.

Carrie: Oh, no problem at all.

Something is Wrong with the Meal

Excuse me, I think I see a hair in my food.

Oh no, I'm so sorry. Would you like a fresh one?

Hi, this pasta seems undercooked.

Really? Would you like a new order?

Excuse me, this soup is so salty that I can't eat it.

Oh sorry, would you like to order something else?

Sorry, I didn't realize this sauce would be so spicy.

Yeah, it's quite spicy! Would you like something else instead?

Hi, I'm just wondering how much longer it will be? I've already been waiting for an hour.

Sorry about that. I'll check with the kitchen right now.

I asked for no mustard on my burger.

Oh no! I'll get the kitchen to make you another one. Sorry about that.

Dialogue #1:

Tom: Hi, excuse me. This soup is way too spicy for me.

Jenny: Oh no. Would you like to try the cream soup instead?

Tom: Sure, is that possible?

Jenny: Yes, it's no problem. I'll bring it right out.

Dialogue #2:

Tim: Excuse me, I ordered my burger with no mayo. But, I think there's some on it.

Carrie: Really? The kitchen must have missed that. Can I get you a fresh one?

Tim: Yes, please. I really hate mayo!

Carrie: No problem. It'll be right up.

Tim: Thank you.

All about the Bill

Hi, could I get the bill, please?

Sure, I'll bring that right over.

Are you paying together or separately?

Together, please.

Separately if possible.

Could you please split the bill?

Sure, no problem.

We are together for the bill, please.

Sure.

Excuse me, I think there's a problem with the bill.

Really? What is it?

Just to let you know, we add a 20% gratuity to the bill for a group of your size.

Okay, thank you.

Dialogue #1:

Tom: Could we get the bill, please?

Jenny: Sure, all together?

Tom: Separately if possible.

Jenny: Of course. No problem.

Tom: Okay great.

Dialogue #2:

Tim: Hi, could we split the bill please?

Carrie: Certainly. Each person is by themselves?

Tim: Yes, except for my wife and I please

Carrie: Okay, I'll change that and be right back.

Tim: Thank you.

Eating Out Review

Write an appropriate response to each statement or question.

What can I get you?

Response:

Would you like to start with a drink?

Response:

Are you interested in dessert?

Response:

Would you like to pay together?

Response:

Can you make this tomato pasta gluten-free?

Response:

What seems to be the problem?

Response:

It'll be about a 30-minute wait.

Response:

Problems and Emergencies

Problems with Cell Phone or Computer

My cell phone isn't working. Do you fix them?

Sure, what kind is it?

I have a MacBook that doesn't turn on. Can you take a look at it?

Sorry, we don't repair Macs.

Yes, you can bring it in. We're open until 6:00 today.

My phone battery isn't working well. Do you replace them?

Yes, we do.

What brand is it?

LG.

I'm wondering if this phone (computer) is under warranty?

Sure, let me take a look. What's the serial number?

I have this old phone that I'm wondering if you can repair.

Let me take a look at it.

I think you'd be better off getting a new one. The repair will be quite expensive.

Dialogue #1:

Tom: Hi, can I help you with something?

Jenny: Yes please. I have this old MacBook that isn't working well anymore.

Tom: What's the problem?

Jenny: It randomly shuts off. I can't figure out why.

Tom: I can take a look at it.

Jenny: Okay, thank you.

Dialogue #2:

Tim: My phone doesn't stay charged for long anymore.

Carrie: Okay, how long does the battery last?

Tim: Only a couple of hours

Carrie: How old is the phone?

Tim: 6 years now.

Carrie: Okay, well we could replace the battery but it might be worth considering a new phone. Most phones these days don't last more than 3 or 4 years. You're lucky to get 6!

Household Appliance Problems

Hi, I'm wondering if you repair ovens?

Sure, what seems to be the problem?

I need some help with my fridge. Could you send someone over?

What's going on with it?

How long has this been happening?

For 2 months now.

Do you repair _____?

Yes, we do.

No, we don't.

When's a good time for us to come?

How about tomorrow afternoon?

How much do you charge?

We charge $50 an hour, with a 2-hour minimum.

Dialogue #1:

Tom: Hi, I'm having some problems with my fridge. Do you repair them?

Jenny: Yes, we do. What seems to be the problem?

Tom: It's not as cold as it used to be, even though it's turned up as high as it goes.

Jenny: How old is it?

Tom: Around 15 years I think.

Jenny: And what brand?

Tom: Samsung.

Jenny: Okay, we can send someone over. Is tomorrow okay for you?

Dialogue #2:

Tim: My oven isn't working well. Could you send someone over to fix it?

Carrie: Sure, what's the problem?

Tim: The stove part works but the oven won't turn on.

Carrie: Okay, I see. What's the make and model?

Tim: It's an LG X3013.

Carrie: It sounds like you need a new heating element. We can send someone over to take a look tomorrow.

Car Problems

Hi, I've been having a few problems with my car. Could you take a look at it?

Sure, how about tomorrow?

What seems to be the problem?

(many answers possible).

Can you bring it in tomorrow?

Sure, that's great. In the afternoon?

What about the day after?

When's the last time you changed/repaired the _____?

Last year.

2 months ago.

What's the make and model?

A 2017 Honda Civic.

Will this be covered by warranty?

Let me check for you. What year is it?

Sorry, brake pads aren't covered under warranty.

Dialogue #1:

Tom: I've been having some problems with the windshield wiper on my car.

Jenny: Okay, how long has it been happening?

Tom: For a few months now.

Jenny: What's the make and model?

Tom: A 20018 Honda Civic.

Jenny: Okay, can you bring it in tomorrow at 1:00?

Tom: Sure, is this covered by warranty?

Jenny: Likely not. This kind of thing usually isn't. I'll know more after I take a look at it.

Dialogue #2:

Tim: I'm wondering if I might need a new battery. It doesn't start that well in the cold.

Carrie: It might be that, or the starter. Want to bring it in and we can take a look?

Tim: Sure, this afternoon is okay?

Carrie: Yes, we're open until 6:00.

Tim: Okay, I'll see you around 2:00.

Feeling Sick

I'm not feeling well right now.

Oh no, what's wrong?

Sorry, I won't be able to come in to work today. I'm not feeling well.

Okay, I hope you feel better.

Sure, keep me updated about tomorrow.

I think I should go see the doctor.

Oh really? What's wrong?

That meal didn't sit quite right.

Oh no. Does your stomach hurt?

I'm feeling a bit sick to my stomach.

Can I do anything to help?

I have a terrible hangover.

Do you need anything?

Did you have a fun night though?

I think I'm coming down with something.

Really? What's wrong?

Dialogue #1:

Tom: Hey Jenny, I'm not feeling well right now.

Jenny: Oh no, what's wrong?

Tom: I know it's my own fault but I have a terrible hangover.

Jenny: I hope you at least had a fun night. Do you need anything?

Tom: Could you grab me some water and an aspirin, please?

Dialogue #2:

Tim: Oh, that Chinese food didn't sit quite right.

Carrie: Oh no! Do you have a stomachache?

Tim: Yes, I feel terrible.

Carrie: Let's stay in tonight.

Tim: That seems like the best plan.

Carrie: Sure, let me know if you need anything.

Tom: I may just take you up on that offer.

Health Emergency

I think I need to go to the hospital.

Really? What's going on?

I think I'm having a heart attack. Call 911.

Okay, I'll do it right now.

Should we call 911?

Yes, I think so.

No, let's drive him to the hospital ourselves. It'll be faster.

I think I broke my leg.

Really? Okay, should I take you to the hospital?

Stay on the phone until the ambulance gets there.

Okay.

How's he doing now?

Worse. His breathing is louder now.

Can you send someone out to meet the ambulance?

Sure, my son will go outside.

How much longer will they be?

They're on their way. It should be about five more minutes.

Dialogue #1:

Tom: I feel terrible. I think I might be having a heart attack.

Jenny: Should we call 911?

Tom: Yes.

Jenny: Okay, I'll do it right now.

Tom: Ugghhhh.

Dialogue #2:

Tim: Are you going into labour? I think we should go to the hospital.

Carrie: Maybe, let me phone my doctor first and see what she says.

Tim: Okay, I'll call her and we can talk to her, okay?

Carrie: Sounds good.

Report a Crime

Hello, what's your emergency?

My house just got broken into.

I just saw a car accident happen.

There's a big fire that just started.

When did it happen?

A couple of minutes ago.

Last night I think.

Where are you?

I'm at _____ .

Who's with you?

Just me.

Stay on the phone until the police get there.

Okay.

Fire, police or ambulance?

Police, please.

Dialogue #1:

Tom: Hi, what's your emergency?

Jenny: I just saw a car accident happen.

Tom: Where are you?

Jenny: At the corner of Green and Oak Street.

Tom: How many cars?

Jenny: 4 cars.

Tom: Okay, stay on the line. I have more questions. Police and ambulance are on their way.

Dialogue #2:

Tim: Hi, I'd like to report some suspicious people near my house.

Carrie: Okay, what are they doing?

Tim: They're just hanging around my neighbor's house. He's away on holidays now. Oh, I think they just went around the back.

Carrie: And you don't know them?

Tim: No, I've never seen them.

Carrie: Okay, what's your neighbor's address? We'll send someone over to check.

Problems and Emergencies Review

Write an appropriate response to each statement or question.

What's your emergency?

Response:

Should we call 911?

Response:

I'm feeling terrible right now.

Response:

My car won't start.

Response:

What seems to the problem?

Response:

How long has this been happening?

Response:

Do you want me to take you to the hospital?

Response:

Who's with you right now?

Response:

131

On the Phone

Ask for Someone

Hi, could I please talk to Jenny?

Sure, I'll put you through.

She's out of the office. Do you want to leave a message?

No, thanks. I'll try later.

Yes, please.

Do you know the extension of the person you're trying to call?

Yes, it's 413.

No, her name is Jenny Ford.

I'd like to talk to someone about _____.

Is this a good time to talk?

Sure.

Actually, can you call back in one hour?

What's your name?

It's Jackie Bolen.

What's your phone number?

It's 743-353-8422.

Dialogue:

Tom: Hi, could I please talk to Jim?

Jenny: Jim Ford?

Tom: Yes, please.

Jenny: Okay, I'll put you through.

Tom: Thank you.

Jenny: He's not answering. Would you like to leave a message?

Tom: Sure, thank you.

Give a Reason for Calling

Hi, I'd like to book an appointment, please.

Sure, with who?

No problem. For when?

I'd like to cancel my appointment, please.

Okay, what's your name?

Sure, what time is it at?

I'd like to order take-out, please.

Sure, what would you like?

What time would you like to pick it up?

What's your name and phone number?

Can I make a reservation, please.

Sure, for what time?

For how many people?

Can I please talk to Jim?

Sure. I'll see if I can find him.

He's not in.

What time will he be back?

Oh, he'll back after lunch in about an hour.

Dialogue #1:

Tom: Hi, I'd like to cancel my appointment, please.

Jenny: Sure, what's the name?

Tom: Tom, for 2:30 tomorrow.

Jenny: Okay, I got it. Would you like to reschedule?

Tom: No thanks. That's okay.

Jenny: Okay, take care.

Dialogue #2:

Tim: Hi, can I put it an order for 12:30 please?

Carrie: Sure, that's for pick-up?

Tim: Yes, please.

Carrie: What would you like?

Tim: 1 combo A and 1 vegetarian combo.

Carrie: Sure, what's your name and phone number?

Tim: Tim. 778-385-2821.

Carrie: Okay, see you at 12:30.

Take or Leave a Message

She's not in right now. Can I take a message?

Sure.

No, thanks. I'll call back later.

No, thanks. Do you know when she'll be in?

Would you like to leave a message?

Yes, please.

No, thanks.

What can I tell him for you?

Please get him to call me back at 423-345-4352.

It's Jackie returning his call.

Can I please leave a message for him?

Sure.

Why don't you try calling back in 30 minutes? He's back from lunch then.

Oh, he's not here? Do you know when he'll be back?

In about an hour.

He's on vacation now. He'll be back next Monday.

Dialogue:

Tom: Can I talk to Jerry, please?

Jenny: He's not in, can I take a message?

Tom: Sure, please tell him it's Tom returning his call.

Jenny: Okay, will do.

Tom: Thank you.

On the Phone Review

Write an appropriate response to each statement or question.

Would you like to leave a message?

Response:

What's your name?

Response:

What's your phone number?

Response:

What can I tell him for you?

Response:

Would you like to reschedule?

Response:

Is now a good time to talk?

Response:

Before You Go

If you found this book useful, please leave a review wherever you bought it. It will help other English learners, like yourself find this resource.

You might also be interested in this book: Advanced English Conversation Dialogues. It has hundreds of helpful English idioms and expressions. Learn to speak more fluently in American English. You can easily find it wherever you like to buy books.

CPSIA information can be obtained
at www.ICGtesting.com
Printed in the USA
BVHW062311130421
604818BV00008B/686